The Cotswolds South
Cheltenham
Stratford upon Avon
Oxford
The Chilterns
Henley on Thames
Bath
Cambridge
London
Belfast
Guernsey
Sark

For information on all our
publications please see
www.cap-ox.co.uk

The Northern Cotswolds

A little souvenir

CHRIS ANDREWS PUBLICATIONS LTD

Crickley Hill and the view to Gloucester

The Cotswolds

INTRODUCTION

For some the name "Cotswolds" conjures a picture of sheltered valleys harbouring villages of honey coloured stone nestling beside clear, fast flowing streams. Others may see the high, bleak open countryside criss-crossed by dry stone walls, or perhaps the bustling old market towns with their fine perpendicular churches. All these views are united by stone; it is oolitic limestone that has created the underlying landscape of the Cotswolds and the buildings for which the area is famed.

On the western edge of the Cotswold escarpment is the 4000 year old Belas Knap, one of the finest long barrows in the country. Its skilfully constructed dry stone walls are the earliest evidence of stonemasonry in an area known for the quality and hue of its stone.

The Romans established a military zone in the Cotswolds, serviced by routes built with stone, some of those remaining are still followed by today's highways. A grass grown amphitheatre and a museum of Roman treasures remind us of the importance of the market town of Cirencester in former times. The Anglo Saxons left little evidence of their rule, other than a legacy of place-

6 The Market Hall, Chipping Campden

names and a few stone churches tucked away in quiet valleys.

Following the Norman conquest of 1066 the church increased in power and wealth, built upon a thriving wool industry. By Domesday in 1086, most of the present day villages existed and an open field system had been created, with vast flocks of sheep grazing on the open sheep walk.

Today's market towns, such as Chipping Campden and Northleach, were founded at this time, built of local stone with the help of masonry skills brought with the Normans. By the 15th century the whole country was so dependent on the wool industry that the Lord Chancellor's seat in the House of Lords came to be known as the woolsack.

Lower Slaughter

The Cotswolds thrived upon the wool trade; wealthy merchants built fine houses and elegant perpendicular churches. Wool processing became increasingly important to the economy; it was initially a cottage industry, but during the 16th century the weaving and fulling became concentrated in the towns and villages of the western Cotswolds where the fast flowing streams from the steep slopes powered the mills.

Between 1700 and 1840, parliamentary intervention, higher taxation and an increase in wool production elsewhere, led to a decline in the Cotswold wool industry and the area paid for an over reliance on the trade. Ironically the rich legacy of 15th and 16th century buildings we see today is partly due to this period of poverty, as there was little money available for new building, although a wealthy minority did build several substantial country houses.

The Cotswolds today reflect their interesting and varied past, and the efforts of many to preserve and maintain their atmosphere. The whole area is designated one of Outstanding Natural Beauty and this little book attempts to show something of its charm. This volume shows the area from north to centre, a sister publication "The Cotswolds South" features the centre to the southern boundary.

Naunton   11

12 Chipping Campden - evening procession after Sir Robert Dover's Games

Chipping Campden from the south   13

14 Broadway Tower, a folly built for Lady Coventry in 1798-99 stands on Fish Hill about Broadway

Broadway Village from the south   15

16   Broadway, sometimes described as the 'show village' of the Cotswolds, seen here on Christmas Eve

Nearby Snowshill is one of the least altered Cotswold villages 17

18   Lavender at the farm just outside Snowshill

20 Different seasons at: Adlestrop, Chipping Campden,

22   Stanton, an attractive small village, sympathetically restored in the early 1900's

Stanway is another small village but with an impressive Jacobean manor house   23

Moreton in Marsh

26   Moreton in Marsh on market day

3 miles north west of Moreton, Blockley's unique collection of buildings reflects its past history of mills and silk production

28   Chastleton House, a rare Jacobean country house, largely unchanged for over 400 years

A classic Cotswold thatched cottage, secreted away in the village of Chastleton 29

30   Stow on the Wold, the highest town in the Cotswolds at 800 feet above sea level

32   The Donnington Brewery south of Stow

Maugersbury 33

34   Temple Guiting, a village owned and named after the Knights Templar in the twelfth century

36 Winchcombe, once a regional capital of Saxon Mercia

Hailes Abbey, founded 1246 by the Duke of Cornwell, son of King John, but ruined at the dissolution of the monasteries

38   Sudeley Castle with a sculpture by Damien Hurst

GENTLEMEN

3205

The GWR Steam Railway at Toddington   39

Cheltenham's Imperial Gardens and statue of Gustav Holst

The Promenade, Cheltenham

42   Pittville Park and Cheltenham College

Sunset over fields near Withington 43

44   Gloucester Cathedral, an original Saxon monastery, rebuilt after 1100

46   Upper Slaughter

Lower Slaughter and the 19th century former corn mill   47

48   Bourton on the Water, sometimes refered to as 'The Venice of the Cotswolds'

The River Windrush and bridges at Bourton 49

50   Great Barrington, Deer Park in winter

52   Charlbury

Shipton under Wychwood   53

54   Blenheim Palace Woodstock, in spring

56   Dawn over Cotswold fields near Burford

58   Woodstock, the stocks in Park Street

60   Virginia creeper at Burford, the town often noted as 'The Gateway to the Cotswolds'

Burford Church and The Hill   61

62 Taynton stone was used throughout the Cotswolds as well as at Oxford, Windsor and London

First published 2005, reprinted 2012, revised and updated 2016, 2017
Chris Andrews Publications Ltd 15 Curtis Yard North Hinksey Lane Oxford OX2 0NA
Telephone: +44(0)1865 723404 email: chris.andrews1@btclick.com. Photos by Chris Andrews,
A. Palmer. W. G. Andrews. All material © Chris Andrews Publications Ltd.
www.cap-ox.com ISBN 978 1 909 759473

Front Cover: Chipping Campden   Title page: Stone carving on Winchcombe Church
This page: Cleeve Hill   Back cover: Bourton on the Water

Chris Andrews

Chris Andrews work is known throughout England and the Channel Islands, and is seen in a variety of publications including calendars, posters, fine art prints and books

This 'Little Souvenir' series attempts to show something of the unique charm of the *Cotswolds Area of Outstanding Natural Beauty* in an attractive and portable form